Cat Out of the Bag

IRENE YATES

Illustrated by Amanda Wood

OXFORD
UNIVERSITY PRESS

OXFORD
UNIVERSITY PRESS

Great Clarendon Street, Oxford OX2 6DP

Oxford University Press is a department of the University of Oxford.
It furthers the University's objective of excellence in research, scholarship,
and education by publishing worldwide in

Oxford   New York

Auckland   Cape Town   Dar es Salaam   Hong Kong   Karachi
Kuala Lumpur   Madrid   Melbourne   Mexico City   Nairobi
New Delhi   Shanghai   Taipei   Toronto

With offices in

Argentina   Austria   Brazil   Chile   Czech Republic   France   Greece
Guatemala   Hungary   Italy   Japan   Poland   Portugal   Singapore
South Korea   Switzerland   Thailand   Turkey   Ukraine   Vietnam

Oxford is a registered trade mark of Oxford University Press
in the UK and in certain other countries

First published 1999
This edition 2005

British Library Cataloguing in Publication Data
Data available

ISBN-13: 978-0-19-918399-9
ISBN-10: 0-19-918399-6

3 5 7 9 10 8 6 4 2

Available in packs
Stage 13 More Stories B Pack of 6:
ISBN-13: 978-0-19-918396-8; ISBN-10: 0-19-918396-1
Stage 13 More Stories B Class Pack:
ISBN-13: 978-0-19-918403-3; ISBN-10: 0-19-918403-8
Guided Reading Cards also available:
ISBN-13: 978-0-19-918405-7; ISBN-10: 0-19-918405-4

Cover artwork by Amanda Wood
Photograph of Irene Yates by Alcester Photography

Printed in Great Britain by
Ashford Colour Press, Gosport Hants

1
Surprise!

Kirandip noticed the cat stretched out in Mrs Weston's kitchen window. It was sleeping in the warmth of the sun.

'You'll never guess!' she said to her mum.

'What's that?' Mum asked.

'Mrs Weston's got a cat!'

Mum shook her head. 'No, that can't be right.'

Kirandip said, 'But I saw it … '

'How can Mrs Weston look after a cat?' said Mum. 'She can't even look after herself!'

That was true. If it wasn't for Mum doing the old lady's shopping, and Kirandip going round next door after school, Mrs Weston would never manage.

Not that Kirandip minded. She had nothing else to do after school anyway – no friends to play with.

She'd had friends at her old school, in London. But that was easy because she had known them for ever. She was at home there.

But Dad had to move here with his job – and Mum and Kirandip had come early, to get her started at the new school.

Now there was no one to play with. No, in nearly a whole term, Kirandip had not found one single friend. Not a proper friend, anyway.

Part of it was because she was shy, she knew that. How she wished …

But what was the point of wishing? She was even too shy to go to the corner shop on her own!

Mum always said, 'Give them a chance, Kirandip. You just have to find something to break the ice ...'

Mum's voice broke into her thoughts. 'Come on, Kirandip! Never mind about cats! Get yourself ready for school – you don't want to be late!'

But, all the same, Kirandip was sure she *had* seen a cat.

She peeped through her bedroom window down into Mrs Weston's back kitchen window. No cat.

Maybe she hadn't seen it after all.

2
It can't be true

All day long Kirandip thought about the cat. She was *sure* she had seen it. A sort of orangey-brown, fluffy thing; fat, with a contented face. It was fast asleep in the window.

She made up her mind to ask Mrs Weston about it.

'It's only me!' Kirandip shouted, letting herself into the entry between the two houses. She banged the gate hard.

Mrs Weston was quite deaf. Kirandip made lots of noise so she wouldn't take her by surprise when she walked in. She didn't want to scare her.

The old lady called through the kitchen. She was always pleased when Kirandip came home from school.

'Hello! Hello, sweetheart! Put the kettle on!'

Kirandip made a pot of tea. She did it every afternoon. Mum was at work until tea-time, so Kirandip always waited for her with Mrs Weston.

No sign of a cat anywhere.

But … there was a saucer of milk on the kitchen floor, at the side of the cooker.

Kirandip caught her breath. She carried the tray to Mrs Weston in the back room.

'Let's have a biscuit,' Mrs Weston said, as she always did. She heaved herself from her chair and across the room to the cupboard.

Kirandip knew better than to offer to help her. Mum always said, 'She's not safe to be here on her own at all really. But you have to let her be independent. She wants to manage by herself!'

Kirandip poured them both a mug of tea.

The old lady offered her the tin of
biscuits. 'Take two, sweetheart,' she said.

Kirandip took a custard cream and a
shortcake. Mrs Weston fussed about,
choosing a ginger nut.

'Tell me what you did at school today.'

'Not much,' said Kirandip. She dipped the custard cream into her mug of tea. 'We had art this afternoon.'

And then she had an idea. 'We painted cats,' she said.

Mrs Weston seemed to give a little jump. She took a long gulp of her tea and paused before she said, 'That's nice. I used to like painting when I was a girl.'

Then, she changed the subject. 'Did you do PE?'

'I painted a black cat,' Kirandip said. She watched the old woman carefully. 'And a tabby.'

The old woman's eyes never left her mug of tea. There was a long silence.

'And then,' said Kirandip, 'I painted an orange one.' She paused.

The air seemed to hold its breath. 'Just like the one that was asleep in your kitchen window this morning.'

The old lady stiffened. She stared at Kirandip.

'What cat?' she said. Her voice somehow seemed to come from far away.

Kirandip nibbled on her biscuit. 'There was a cat in your kitchen. This morning. In the window,' she said. Then, she added, 'All stretched out. Fast asleep.'

'Oh no,' said Mrs Weston, shaking her head. 'You've made a mistake. There's no cat here!' She laughed, a bit nervously, Kirandip thought.

Kirandip thought hard. She *had* seen the cat. She knew it. But she couldn't accuse the old lady of telling lies; could she?

'Well,' she said, at last, 'I thought I did. But if you say I didn't ...' She paused.

Mrs Weston clicked her teeth. 'You couldn't have, could you?' she said. She picked up her mug. 'Let's have another cup of tea. And you can tell me what you did in PE.'

She's hiding something, Kirandip thought. *I didn't say we did PE. She's trying to change the subject again.*

Kirandip put the teapot and the mugs on the tray and went to go into the little kitchen. That was when she heard the noise. *Miaow.*

It seemed to be coming from behind
the door into the front room. *Miaow!*
There it was again!

Kirandip glanced quickly at Mrs Weston. But the old lady couldn't hear the noise at all. She was smiling at Kirandip and pointing into the kitchen.

'Go on, sweetheart! Kettle on!'

And then it came again. *Miaow!*

Suddenly Mrs Weston seemed to guess why Kirandip was standing still.

'What is it?' she said, anxiously. 'What's the matter?'

'I can hear a noise,' Kirandip said. 'It's coming from the front room. And it's a cat ... crying!'

All the colour drained out of Mrs Weston's face.

'You can hear it?' she asked, nervously.

Kirandip nodded.

Mrs Weston seemed to shrink even further into her chair. She stared down at her hands. 'Oh dear,' she said. 'Now everybody will find out. Now I'll get in trouble! And then they'll get rid of me!'

Kirandip stared at the old lady,
horrified. What did she mean – *get rid
of her*?

The old lady began to cry. 'You're not
supposed to have pets here! It's not my
fault! The cat just came! I couldn't turn
it away! It likes me! But if the landlord
finds out, I'll be done for!'

'They can't get rid of you just because
you've got a cat!' Kirandip said, upset.

'Can't they!' Angrily, the old lady drew herself up in her chair. 'You don't know what they do to old people!'

Her face was red; her eyes smouldered with angry fire. 'Nobody wants you when you're old! You'll see!'

Kirandip's mouth opened and stayed open. Mrs Weston couldn't be right. She just couldn't.

'And anyway,' the old lady continued, 'it's even worse than that! You don't know the half!'

Kirandip was puzzled. 'What half?'

Suddenly, the old lady collapsed back into her chair. 'I don't know what I'm going to do,' she said, sobbing. 'The cat's having kittens.'

3

Sworn to secrecy

The cat was a beautiful tortoiseshell.

'Tortoiseshells are always queens,' Mrs Weston told Kirandip. She stroked the cat gently as it curled up on her lap.

'Stripy, ginger ones are nearly all toms. That means they're boys. But the patterned, orange ones are always girls.

'She's a lovely cat. And somebody must have thrown her out – because of the kittens.'

'What's her name?'

'I don't know what her real name is. I just call her Kitty,' said Mrs Weston.

Kirandip bit her lip. Already she could see how much the old lady loved the cat.

'What do you feed her on?'

Tight-lipped, the old lady said, 'She has to share my dinner. I can't get to the shop, can I? And I couldn't ask your mum to get me any cat food, otherwise she'd know.

'So Kitty eats what I eat. She's very hungry. But that's because of her babies.'

'When do you think they'll come?' asked Kirandip.

The old lady shook her head. 'I'm not sure,' she said, 'but it won't be long now. Listen. You *are* my friend, aren't you? The cat has got to be our secret. You won't tell anybody, will you?' Her eyes gleamed. 'Because if you do …'

Kirandip was saved from answering by the sound of the back gate. 'It must be Mum!'

'Quick!' hissed Mrs Weston. 'Get Kitty into the front room!'

Kirandip grabbed the cat and raced for the door into the front room.

The cat gave a little howl of protest as it was shoved through into the other room. Kirandip's heart missed a beat. *Please don't let Mum hear her!*

'Hellooah!' Mum called out as she came in through the kitchen.

'Hello, Surinder,' sang Mrs Weston in
an unruffled way; for all the world as
though nothing had happened.

Mum looked at them both.

'Everything all right?' she asked.

21

They both nodded, avoiding each other's eyes. Mum gave them a long, cool glance. 'Good,' she said at last.

Kirandip was *sure* she suspected something.

There was a bit of a silence and then Mum said, 'Come on then, Kirandip. I'm making samosas. You can help. You can bring some round for Mrs Weston later. Come and get your school clothes off ...'

Just as she was going out, Kirandip had an idea. 'I've got to go down to the corner shop for Mrs Weston,' she said, brightly.

For a moment, Mum's eyes held a look of surprise. 'But …' she began. There was a pause, and then she said, 'Okay, but hurry up – it will soon be dark.' And off she went.

Mrs Weston said, 'I didn't ask you to get anything from the shop!'

'I know you didn't,' answered Kirandip. 'But I thought it would be a good idea to go and get some proper cat food, for Kitty.'

And for some reason she wasn't scared in the least.

4

Rules are rules

Kirandip couldn't really believe that someone could be thrown out of their house just for keeping a cat.

She wished she had someone to ask at school. But who? It wasn't exactly the sort of thing she could start asking in class. They'd think she was mad.

She decided she would ask her dad when he came up from London at the weekend.

When he came home, Kirandip
wasted no time.

'Dad, can we have a pet?'

Mr Singh looked over the top of the
newspaper he was reading.

'A pet, Kiri? What do you mean –
a pet? You're at school all day, and your
mother is at work in the hospital. And
I am in London.'

He laughed, a kind laugh. 'No. It's not
a good idea to have a pet. Who would
look after it?'

'But could we have one if we wanted
one? A dog? A cat?'

Mr Singh put down his paper. 'Well, that's difficult, Kiri. I don't think we're supposed to have animals in this house.'

'Why?'

He shrugged. 'Because the landlord says so. Perhaps he doesn't like them. Perhaps he's worried about fleas and things. I don't know.'

'What would happen if we got one and we didn't tell him?'

Mr Singh grinned wickedly.

'I think we would probably have to look for a new house!' he said. Then he chuckled to himself, and picked up his newspaper again.

So it was true. Kirandip swallowed hard. She didn't know what to do. She couldn't possibly tell her mum and dad the secret.

And she knew Mrs Weston wouldn't send the cat away, especially with the kittens due. She was bound to get found out one day.

But before that happened, there was
suddenly a lot more than one cat to
worry about.

5

The birth day

On Wednesday afternoon, Mrs Weston was waiting anxiously by the entry gate when Kirandip got home from school.

'Quick! Quick!' she hissed. 'Oh, my goodness! What a terrible day I've had!' She clutched at Kirandip's arm and began to pull her into the house.

Kirandip's heart did a little jump. What had happened?

'The kittens!' whispered the old lady. 'She's had the kittens!' She bulldozed Kirandip into the front room.

Kirandip had never been in there before. Her eyes widened. The room looked just like a picture she'd seen in a history book at school – all brown and gloomy.

There was a huge old armchair in the window.

'That's my Bill's armchair,' Mrs Weston said, catching her looking at it. 'He always used to sit in the window and watch what was going on.'

The room had a damp, musty smell; not like the front room in Kirandip's house, which was all pink and pretty and smelled of *pot pourri*.

Kirandip couldn't see Kitty anywhere.

'There!' hissed Mrs Weston. She pointed to a rickety glass cabinet, full of old cups and plates.

Kirandip looked again.

Kitty was there all right, curled up, tucked right underneath it.

It looked as though she had squeezed in and made some sort of a little nest. She was in a cardboard box that was squashed underneath the cabinet.

The cat gave Kirandip a startled look, as if to say, 'Don't you dare come near me!'

Kirandip stretched out her hand. She bent down and made a little mewing noise. 'It's all right, Kitty,' she murmured, 'I'm not going to hurt you.'

The cat just stared right at her.

Then Kirandip saw something move.
A tiny kitten poked its little head out
from underneath its mother's body. It
gave a little cry.

The kitten looked as if it hadn't any fur and its eyes were tightly closed. 'Oh!' gasped Kirandip.

Mrs Weston's voice boomed in Kirandip's ear. 'Seven! That's what she's had! Seven kittens!'

Seven! Oh no, thought Kirandip. That was the cat out of the bag then! How on earth could they keep them secret? One cat they could manage. But eight ...?

No chance!

6

More trouble!

'I'm sure Kiri and our neighbour are up to something!' Kirandip heard her mum's voice speaking to her dad over the phone. 'She's round there all the time. I have to keep calling her to come home. *And* she keeps going to the corner shop ...'

Kirandip sat on the stairs to listen.

'How do I know what they're up to?' Mum said. 'But I'll tell you one thing. You must try and get to the bottom of it when you get home on Friday – because I can't!'

Oh no! Kirandip crept away back upstairs to her bedroom.

She knew that if her dad started to ask her what was going on, in the end she would give in and tell him. He had that kind of way with her.

She could be vague with her mum and make all kinds of excuses – she never told her *lies*. But she couldn't get round her dad. He always seemed to be able to get the truth out of her.

'I don't know what we're going to do!' Kirandip told Mrs Weston.

The kittens – two ginger toms, three tortoiseshells and two grey and brown stripy ones – were getting bigger.

To tell the truth, they were beginning to be a bit of a nuisance.

They were almost five weeks old now.

Kitty was worn out. The little ones kept racing after her, jumping up to drink milk. They clung on to her no matter how hard she tried to shake them off.

The old lady and Kirandip had tried to get them to lap milk and bread from a saucer, but they wouldn't have it.

Kirandip had fetched a litter tray and packets of litter from the corner shop. She had tried not to let her mum see her. But even that had turned out to be a mistake.

For a start, it wasn't very easy to train the kittens; they had accidents everywhere. The tray had to stay in the front room so that Mum wouldn't see it. The front room smelled horrible.

Also, because the tray was too heavy for Mrs Weston, Kirandip had to keep emptying it in the outside bin. *Phew!*

And every afternoon, when Mum came round to fetch her, Mrs Weston had to find an excuse to hurry them both out of the house. She didn't want Kirandip's mum to have time to smell the pong, or hear the kittens chasing about in the front room.

But Kirandip knew they couldn't go on like that for ever. Maybe she would have to tell her dad on Friday when he came home, after all.

But suppose she did, and he told the landlord? Suppose the landlord came round and ordered Mrs Weston out?

If he did, where would poor Mrs Weston go?

7
Disaster!

Kirandip worried about it for the whole week.

She didn't mind talking to people since she'd been going to the corner shop. So she wondered whether she should ask in class if anybody wanted a kitten.

She began to tell Sophie, a girl in her class, but then she decided against it. Suppose they all came knocking on the door, asking to see them? How would she explain *that* to Mum?

On Friday afternoon, she rushed to
Mrs Weston's as usual. But when she got
there, there was no, *Hello! Hello,
sweetheart! Put the kettle on!*

'It's only me!' Kirandip shouted, as
she let herself in.

Nothing. No sound. *Where was Mrs
Weston?*

And then Kirandip heard something
that made her heart stop. It was a low
moaning sound. And it was coming
from the front room.

Kirandip rushed through the open door, stepping over scrabbling, mewling kittens on her way.

Kitty looked up at her with weary eyes, from high up on the back of Mrs Weston's Bill's chair.

She seemed to say, 'I've had about enough of this. Look what they've done now!' And then Kirandip saw Mrs Weston.

She was lying in a heap in front of the
fireplace. She was all muddled up with
the brass fire irons, and the cardboard
box from under the cabinet.

The litter tray was spilled all around
her.

'Sweetheart! Sweetheart! I've had a
little fall ...' Mrs Weston managed to
gasp. 'Help me. Help ...' And then she
took one deep breath and her eyes
closed in her ashen, white face.

Kirandip's stomach did somersaults. *Was the old lady dead? What was she to do?*

Around her, the kittens leapt and scampered and scurried, catching each other's tails in their teeth.

They looked as if there was nothing else to do in the world but play.

Kirandip remembered fainting once. She'd been at the shops with her mum. She'd gone really hot and felt wobbly and then, suddenly, she fainted.

All she remembered about it was water being splashed on her face and coming to, sitting in the shop manager's office.

Perhaps Mrs Weston had just fainted.

Quickly, she rushed into the kitchen and found a bowl. She filled it with water, and grabbed the tea-towel from the draining board.

Then she scuttled back into the front
room, trying not to step on any of the
kittens as she went.

They were still jumping about, as
though there was nothing wrong.

Kirandip knelt down beside her
friend. *'Please,'* she whispered, *'please!'*

She could feel her heart thumping as
she pressed the tea-towel into the bowl
of water, squeezed it out, and smoothed
it on to Mrs Weston's face. *'Please! Please!'*

Suddenly, the old lady stirred. She gave a little sigh and stroked her tongue across her lips.

Kirandip dipped her fingers into the water and held them to Mrs Weston's mouth. Her eyes flickered open.

'Stay there!' Kirandip said – thinking even as she said it what a silly thing it was to say! She raced into the kitchen for a cup of water.

She put her arm under the old lady's head and lifted it. Then she held the cup of water to her mouth.

In a few minutes, Mrs Weston was feeling much better. The colour came back into her cheeks.

Kirandip got a glare from Kitty as she took away her cushions, but she took them just the same. Kirandip managed to prop up Mrs Weston with Kitty's cushions, and some more from Bill's chair.

'What happened?' asked Kirandip.

Mrs Weston gave a huge sigh. 'Thought I'd get Kitty away from the kittens for a rest. When I came in they were all under my feet. I tried to shoo them away.' Mrs Weston paused.

'Kitty must have thought I was attacking her babies. She rushed at me. I thought she was going to bite me. I put my arm out to stop her and – whoosh! Over the litter tray I went! And then I couldn't get up!'

'Well, you mustn't even try,' said Kirandip, seriously. 'You might have broken something. We'll just have to wait here, till Mum comes.' She looked at her friend, anxiously. 'Perhaps I should get an ambulance …'

'Oh no, no, no,' said Mrs Weston, crossly. 'I'm not going anywhere in any ambulance. But you'll have to sort the cats out – before your mum gets here. I know. Take them upstairs. You can shut them in the bedroom.'

Kirandip stared at her. Didn't the old lady understand? It was all over. She couldn't keep the cats a secret any longer. 'But ...' Kirandip started to say.

'No buts about it, sweetheart,' said Mrs Weston, her voice suddenly harsh. 'You've got to hide the cats. Otherwise they'll know. And then ...' She lowered her voice and spoke in the most woeful tone Kirandip had ever heard, 'they'll get rid of me!'

8
Taking charge

Kirandip sat on the floor, thinking about how she could collect the kittens. She'd have to carry them two at a time. She'd have to take them up the stairs and shut them in a room.

Then she'd have to come back down and get some more. But how would she stop the first lot getting out of the room while she was putting in the second lot? They were so fast, and so full of energy …

Then there was Kitty herself. It didn't
seem right to move her. She was so
comfortable on the back of Mrs
Weston's Bill's chair.

Besides, she wouldn't take kindly to
Kirandip picking her up.

Come to that, she wouldn't be very
happy about Kirandip taking the kittens.

Suppose Kitty thought she was trying
to steal them? Suppose Kitty went for
her the same way she'd gone for Mrs
Weston?

It was not going to be easy.

'You'd better hurry up, sweetheart,'
Mrs Weston said, 'because your mum
will be here in a minute. What if she
finds us in this pickle? What are we
going to do?'

'But what are we going to say,'
Kirandip wailed, 'when she asks us
what happened?'

Mrs Weston looked at Kirandip,
blankly. 'We'll just have to say I fell,'
she suggested.

'Yes,' said Kirandip. 'But what
about ...' She waved her arm at the
cat litter everywhere. 'What about all
this mess?'

It was impossible to clean it up before her mum came home, Kirandip knew that.

And then, another thought struck her.

She heard her mum's voice in her head. *'She's not safe to be here on her own really.'*

It's true, Kirandip thought. She's not. And how can she stay here with eight cats? I can't keep coming round here, cleaning up after them – not eight of them.

And what's she going to do when they start growing up?

What if the kittens start having babies?

What if all the female kittens had kittens of their own, and then those kittens had kittens, and then ... It didn't take a lot of working out.

Before you could turn round there would be hundreds of cats in the house. And even Mrs Weston couldn't cope with that, no matter how independent she wanted to be!

Suddenly, Kirandip knew what she had to do.

'Right,' she said, taking charge. 'I'm going to make you a cup of tea. Then I'll tidy up a bit. Then,' she said, her mind made up, 'we'll wait for Mum and we're going to tell her *exactly* what has happened!'

Mrs Weston's face crumpled. 'I thought you were my friend,' she said sulkily. 'But you're not. You're just the same as them. You want to get rid of me as well.'

9

Found out

Mum's face was a picture when she
walked into the kitchen and had to step
over the frisky kittens. 'What's all this?'

Breathlessly, Kirandip began to tell her
the story.

'There was this cat. And Mrs Weston
said the landlord would get rid of her if
he found out. Then the kittens came.
And then we had to get a litter tray. And
then she fell over. And then …'

Mum's face turned chalky. 'Who fell? Who?' she demanded. Before Kirandip could answer she had rushed into the front room.

There was Mrs Weston, still in a heap on the floor, dabbing away at the tears that rolled down her cheeks.

'Now then, now then!' Mum told her. 'Let's see if anything is broken.'

Briskly, she felt Mrs Weston for broken bones. When she was sure nothing was wrong, she helped her to her feet and sat her in Bill's chair.

'You did very well, Kirandip,' she said, 'to keep Mrs Weston where she was. Well done. I'm sure there's nothing broken. It is probably shock more than anything. Now then, about these cats ...'

Mrs Weston began to weep again.

'She thinks the landlord will throw her out of the house,' explained Kirandip, 'because of the cats.'

'Oh, what nonsense!' said Mum, haughtily. 'Your father will see to it when he gets home.'

Kirandip drew in her breath. 'Do you think so? Really?'

'Of course,' replied her mother. 'There is nothing my Ranjit cannot do. Now – how about that tea you were making?'

10

A good move

It was true. Dad had not been home
long before he began to sort things out.

First, he phoned the landlord.

'We've changed the rules now! I don't
mind the old lady having one cat!' he
laughed. 'One cat is not too bad!'

Then he said to Dad, 'If she's not safe in the house, I have an empty flat she could have. It's just along the road, by the corner shop. No stairs. She would be better off in that! And I could use her house for a family.'

They all went round to see Mrs Weston. Dad told her what the landlord said. 'Then,' he continued, 'you'd be much safer. There's a lady on the top floor who could keep an eye on you. We could help you move in!'

Mrs Weston's eyes glistened. 'He wants to get rid of me!'

'Oh no!' Dad said. 'You don't *have* to go. He just made the offer!'

Mrs Weston thought for a moment. She said, 'What about my Bill's chair?'

'I'm sure it would fit in, right by the window,' said Dad.

'What about Kitty?' asked Mrs Weston.

'Kitty can go with you. I can put a cat flap in the kitchen door so she can go in and out when she pleases!' Dad said.

Mrs Weston seemed to perk up slightly. 'But what about her babies?'

Mum said, 'I think that it would be a good idea to advertise them. Kiri could put a notice in the corner shop – couldn't she?'

'Perhaps we could keep one for ourselves!' Kirandip said, hopefully.

Dad looked as if he were about to protest, but Mum gave him a look and he thought better of it. 'Well ...'

'I could ask at school if anybody wants one!' Kirandip said, excitedly.

'Good idea!' said Mum.

Mrs Weston said, 'If I moved, would you still come and see me?'

'Every day – just as usual,' said Kirandip. She meant it.

Mrs Weston had been her first friend in her new home and if it hadn't been for her, and the cat, and the kittens …

But, for the moment, Kirandip was busy. She was working out exactly what her notices in the shop and at school would say.

Kirandip's heart sang. If that didn't break the ice, nothing would.

About the author

I remember when I was little, telling a story I'd made up about crocodiles at a party. I knew then that I wanted to be a writer. I used to write stories at school and pass them round class. I was always in trouble for it. If I was stuck on a desert island, I wouldn't care as long as I had lots of pencils and paper.

The idea for this story came when a friend rescued a cat that was having kittens. I thought, what if the kittens had kittens, and then they had kittens …